KUNDALINI:
THE MOTHER-POWER

SRI CHINMOY

KUNDALINI:
THE MOTHER-POWER

SRI CHINMOY

Cover design by Ashok

ISBN 0-88497-104-X

Printed by: Agni Press, 84-47 Parsons Blvd., Jamaica, N.Y. 11432

INTRODUCTION

In this rare book, a fully illumined spiritual Master explains different techniques for awakening the Kundalini and opening the third eye and other chakras. As one who has experienced the whole range of Kundalini Power, Sri Chinmoy warns of dangers and pitfalls to be avoided and discusses some of the occult powers that come with the opening of the chakras. He speaks of ways to tell if the chakras are opening, the relationship between Kundalini and the Divine Mother and, most important, the world beyond the Kundalini experience. The book consists of four significant talks and Sri Chinmoy's answers to a number of specific questions he has been asked on the subject.

YOU ARE MY OCEAN, MOTHER

Mother, You respond to my song;
Therefore I sing.
Your Affection is boundless, Mother,
    I know.
Even when I forget You through my sulking,
Your Infinite Compassion and Peace
    draw me toward You.
You are my ocean, Mother; I am Your
    tiniest drop.
The stars, the moon and the sun
    are all Your eternal companions
In Your Cosmic Game.

                                    — Sri Chinmoy

TABLE OF CONTENTS

Sri Chinmoy was invited by Dr. James Carse, Chairman of the Religion Department at New York University, to give a series of lectures on Kundalini Yoga on consecutive Wednesday evenings beginning February 14, 1973. Sri Chinmoy offers his deepest blessing to Nilaya [Mr. David Gershon], who made the arrangements for this series of talks.

THE MOTHER ASPECT OF
THE DIVINE

God is both Mother and Father to us; He is both masculine and feminine. The Kundalini power is the power of the Supreme Goddess, the power of the Mother aspect of the Divine. Sometimes the Mother wants to play with Her children who like to see their Mother's Power; or sometimes, in order to see the strength of Her children, She plays all kinds of games. Then She comes down to the children's level to show them how much power and strength they can get if they behave well, if they do well. The children are charmed; they are fascinated. They feel, "Mother is so strong; Mother is so powerful."

The Mother has to come down considerably in order to show Her Kundalini Power.

She shows some miracles and the children want to learn how to do it. The Mother says, "All right, first learn this kind of game." Then She shows her highest Power, highest Consciousness. At that time the children are dumbfounded. They say, "O, Mother is like that!" Then they start practising love, devotion and surrender. When they see the Mother in Her highest Form, which is Her real Form, then they feel that these Kundalini powers are nothing. They are like playing with little flames and fires.

Kundalini power is power, true; but it has a tremendous restlessness. Kundalini power is most of the time like a monkey; its quality is restlessness. But real spiritual power, the Supreme Mother's Power from the highest level, is not restless. When we use spiritual power and offer peace, it is real peace.

Even if we use Kundalini powers for the right purpose, we won't be able to offer infinite Peace, infinite Bliss, infinite Light that way. No matter how many miracles we show, the person who sees them will be pleased for only five minutes and then he will be jealous because he does not have this power. Then, when we do not show him the power the next time, he becomes mad and doubts. He will think that we have limited capacity, that we can do miracles only from time to time. Kundalini power can perform all kinds of miracles; but when it is a matter of elevating someone's consciousness, it won't be able to elevate the consciousness even one inch. For that we need spiritual power, the power that comes from the Supreme Goddess at Her highest level.

KUNDALINI YOGA:
THE MOTHER-POWER

Do we want to follow the path of Kundalini Yoga? Then we must not sleep. We must not sleep in the world of darkness and night. The world of darkness weakens our inner potentialities. The world of night destroys our outer possibilities. When our inner potentialities are weakened, our life becomes miserable. When our outer possibilities are destroyed, our life becomes unbearable. Where can our inner potentialities safely grow? Our inner potentialities can safely grow only in the heart of the Mother-Power, Kundalini. When can our outer possibilities be effective? Our outer possibilities can be effective only when we are at the feet of the Mother-Power, Kundalini.

Do we want to follow the path of Kundalini Yoga? Then we must possess an adamantine will. We must be brave in the world of ignorance and inconscience. Ignorance compels us to be helpless and useless. When we feel useless, the Mother-Power in us feels helpless. When we feel helpless, the Mother-Power in us untiringly encourages, inspires and illumines us out of Her infinite Compassion.

Do we want to follow the path of Kundalini Yoga? Then we must love. We must love the Mother in us, love the Mother before us and love the Mother around us. The Mother in us is soulful. The Mother before us is beautiful. The Mother around us is powerful. We need the Mother of Soul to play the Cosmic Game of Life. We need the Mother of Beauty to sing the Cosmic Song of Life. We need the Mother of Power to dance the Cosmic Dance of Life. The Game of Life energises us. The Song of Life enlightens us. The Dance of Life immortalises us. Our energy is for the world to use. Our enlightenment is for the world to glorify. Our immortality is for the world to treasure.

Do we want to follow the path of Kundalini Yoga? Then Power must come first in our life and Power must come last in our life. When Power divine is our first choice, fear leaves us. When Power divine is our last choice, doubt leaves us. When fear leaves us, we become what we wanted to be: divine warriors. When doubt leaves us, we become what we originally were: the Universal Self.

Do we want to follow the path of Kundalini Yoga? Then we have to feel that each second of our life is as important as a whole year. And we have to realise that each year is filled with as many opportunities as there are seconds. Each second carries us either toward realisation or toward frustration. Each year carries us either toward the transcendental Truth or toward the abysmal falsehood.

Truth tells us that we are God's chosen children. We need God to reach the Highest and God needs us to manifest the Highest. Falsehood tells us that we are death's instruments and that death needs us badly. The transcendental Truth beckons us. The abysmal falsehood frightens us. When the transcendental Truth beckons us, we feel that we are none other than the Supreme. When the abysmal falsehood frightens us, we feel that we are the eternal slaves of ignorance, inconscience and death.

Do we want to follow the path of Kundalini Yoga? Then we need purity in thought and purity in action. With a pure thought, we build the strongest and largest palace of love and fulfilment. With an impure thought, we break down and demolish the strongest and largest palace of love and fulfilment. We give birth to a pure and divine thought when we feel that we are of God and for God. We give birth to an impure, undivine thought when we feel that we are of ignorance unknowable and for ignorance known and unknown. With a pure action we become the life-saver of the aspiring world. With an impure action we become the life-destroyer of the entire world.

Do we want to follow the path of Kundalini Yoga? Then we have to know that our essence is the Delight-power of Heaven and our existence is the Peace-power for earth. With the Delight-power we begin. With the Peace-power we end.

February 14, 1973

PRANA AND THE
POWER OF THE CHAKRAS

Kundalini Yoga is the Yoga of prana. Prana is the life-energy or life-principle of the universe. There are three principal channels through which this life-energy flows. These channels are ida, pingala and sushumna. In Sanskrit these channels are called nadis. Ida, pingala and sushumna are inside our subtle physical body, not inside the gross physical. Ida carries the current of life-energy in the left side of the body. Pingala carries the current in the right side of the body. Sushumna carries the current in the middle of the spinal column. Sushumna is the most important of the three nadis. It receives a ceaseless stream of life-energy from the universal Consciousness-light. There is an inner connection between ida and pingala and the zodiac and planets. Ida has a special connection with the moon and the planet Mercury; hence its main quality is coolness and mildness. Pingala is connected with the sun and Mars; hence its quality is powerful and dynamic heat.

Ida rules the left nostril. Pingala rules the right nostril. When we breathe in and out primarily through our left nostril, we have to know that it is ida that is functioning. When we breathe in and out through our right nostril, it is pingala that is functioning. And when both of our nostrils are functioning satisfactorily, we have to know that it is sushumna that is playing its role. It also happens at times that ida breathes in and pingala breathes out.

Ida, pingala and sushumna meet together at six different places. Each meeting place forms a centre and each centre is round like a wheel. Indian spiritual philosophy calls these centres chakras. They are also called lotuses, because they look like the lotus flower. The six centres, as perhaps you know, are muladhara, svadhisthana, manipura, anahata, vishuddha and ajna. There is also another chakra that is inside the brain, called sahasrara. Because it is in the brain, and not along the spinal column, it is not counted with the other six centres. Apart from these six, there are many other chakras in the subtle physical body. Here in the knee we have a chakra; even in the toes and the fingertips we have chakras. But these chakras are minor and are not usually mentioned.

The root chakra, or the lotus muladhara, has four petals, which are red and orange in colour. The spleen chakra, svadhisthana, has six petals. The petals are orange, blue, green, yellow, violet and blood-red. Blood-red is the most prominent colour in this chakra. The navel chakra, manipura, has ten petals. They are pink, orange and green, but primarily green. The heart chakra, anahata, has twelve petals. Here the colour is bright golden. The throat centre, the vishuddha lotus, has sixteen petals. Blue and green are the colours. The brow centre, ajna, has only two petals. But inside each petal there are forty-eight petals. Here the colour is rose. The crown centre, sahasrara, has 1,000 petals, or to be more precise, 972. It has all the colours, but the violet colour is predominant.

The universal Consciousness embodies universal Music. From each chakra, where the life-energy from the universal Consciousness gathers, a musical note is produced. From sahasrara the tone of shadja or sa is produced. In western music, you call this 'do'. From ajna, rishava or ri is produced: what you call 're'. From vishuddha, gandhara or ga is produced: what you call 'mi'. From anahata, madhyama or ma is produced: what you call 'fa'. From manipura, panchama or pa is produced: what you call 'so'. From svadhisthana, dhaivata or dha is produced: what you call 'la'. From muladhara, nishada or ni is produced: what you call 'ti'.

There are seven worlds corresponding to the seven chakras. Muladhara corresponds to Bhurloka; svadhisthana corresponds to Bhubarloka; manipura corresponds to Svarloka; anahata corresponds to Janaloka; vishuddha corresponds to Tapoloka; ajna corresponds to Maharloka; and sahasrara corresponds to Satyaloka. Each world is symbolised by something. Bhurloka is symbolised by earth, Bhubarloka by water, Svarloka by heat, Janaloka by air, Tapoloka by ether, Maharloka by energy, and Satyaloka by infinite space.

For each centre there is a special Mother-Power, which is a manifestation of the Supreme Mother. These Mother-Powers are

8

known as Brahmi, Parameshwari, Kaumari, Vaishnavi, Varahi, Indrani and Chamunda. Each one has a special place of her own. Brahmi is the Mother-Power that embodies and pervades the infinite space. She rules all the chakras. Brahmi stays in the sahasrara, or brain chakra, which is the thousand-petaled lotus. From there she rules the centres that are below her: ajna, vishuddha, anahata, manipura, svadisthana and muladhara. Parameshwari is located in the ajna chakra, the brow centre. There she rules ajna and the chakras that are below her. Kaumari is located in vishuddha, the throat centre, and rules vishuddha and the chakras below her. Vaishnavi begins functioning from anahata, the heart centre, and rules the others below. Varahi, who stays in the navel centre, rules the lower planes: manipura, svadhisthana and muladhara. Indrani rules svadhisthana, at the spleen, and muladhara, at the base of the spine. And Chamunda rules only over muladhara.

Each centre also has a presiding deity, a cosmic god. Brahma is the presiding deity of muladhara; Rudra is the presiding deity of svadhisthana; Vishnu, of manipura; Ishwara, of anahata; Sadashiva, of vishuddha; Shambhu, of ajna; and Para-mashiva is the presiding deity of sahasrara.

These centres can be opened in various ways. The usual method for those who practise Kundalini Yoga is to concentrate firmly on each centre, invoking the Mother-Power or the presiding deity most soulfully. However, all real spiritual Masters, from the very depth of their experience, say that it is better to open the heart centre first and then try to open the other centres. If one opens the heart centre first, there is prac-tically no risk. But if one starts with the muladhara or svadhisthana or ajna chakra, it is very dangerous. Again, there are some seekers who do not follow this method at all. They do not care for occult power; they care only for God's Love, Light and Truth. They learn how to meditate most soulfully; and when they make considera-ble progress in their meditation, these centres open automatically. And through the Grace of the Absolute Supreme, these centres may open even without meditation.

If these centres are opened without proper purification, the seeker will encoun-ter great pain. It will be like playing with fire or a sharp knife. He may destroy others or he may himself be destroyed. We have to know that the miraculous powers that one gets when his centres are opened are not actually miraculous or unusual at all in the inner world. The powers that the centres hold are absolutely normal. In the inner world these powers are constantly used by spiritual Masters. There in the inner world they are normal and natural. Only when they are used on the physical plane do they seem unusual or miraculous.

Any real spiritual Master will have these powers. But again, one need not be a spiritual Master of the highest order in order to have them. One need not be even a great seeker. Even someone who leads a normal, ordinary, undivine life can develop these powers.

In India I came across a few seekers — I cannot call them sincere seekers — who had some occult or kundalini power. But most of the time they misused it. They opened their third eye in order to know what their girlfriends were thinking of them. Now this is ridiculous. The same third eye they could have used to destroy their dark, obscure, impure thoughts. They had the capacity, but they didn't use it. I also know someone who used his occult power to threaten his enemies at night and compel them to do whatever he wanted them to do the following morning. By using his occult power, his third eye, he made his enemies his slaves. But he could have used his third eye to know God's Will in his own life and in others' lives. If it had been God's Will to expedite somebody's spiritual progress, then he could have used his third eye to help. Each centre has something special to offer when it is properly used. It becomes a veritable boon to the Inner Pilot and to all mankind.

I want to make it very clear that the opening of the centres does not mean that one is realising God or that he is about to realise God. The opening of the centres is not necessarily the precursor of God-realisation. No, not at all! God-realisation has nothing to do with the opening of the centres. No matter how many centres one has opened, even if one has opened all the seven centres, it does not indicate that one is on the verge of realisation or that one is realised. From the highest spiritual point of view, the opening of the chakras is like the games a mother plays with her children in the playground. Children are fond of games and the mother is showing her capacity. It is not her pride, her vanity. No. It is just that the mother knows this will amuse the children. She can give some joy, some pleasure to the children, so she plays these games. It is usually Lord Shiva on the sahasrara plane and his consort, Shivani, from the muladhara plane, where the kundalini is fast asleep, who play. When they play with their children in the inner world, the occult powers start functioning.

Now let us start from the beginning: muladhara, the root chakra. When one has acquired mastery over the muladhara centre, one can become invisible at his sweet will. One can conquer all diseases. One can know whatever one wants to know and discover whatever one wants to discover. If one wants to discover God's Compassion, God's Light, God's Love for him, then he is in a position to do so. But if one uses the same power in order to know what is happening in others' minds or what is going on in their outer life, or if one uses it to discover out of curiosity if a third world war is going to break out, then this power is misused.

When a person with mastery over the muladhara sees that someone has a particular disease, he has to know whether that individual deserves the disease or whether it is the result of a hostile attack. If he has done something wrong, naturally under the law of karma he deserves to pay the penalty. But if the disease is not from the law of karma but rather from the attack of some hostile force, and if it is God's Will that his disease should be cured, then naturally a spiritual person who has the capacity should cure it. But if he does it at his own sweet will, or if he acts in an undivine way and just shows off, then he breaks the cosmic law. He will cure the person but this very cure will act eventually against both the healer and the sick person. It will add to their ignorant and self-destructive quality. So the healer has to know if it is the Will of God that the person be cured. Only then will he cure; otherwise he has to remain silent and do nothing. You may ask, how can he see somebody else suffering and still do nothing? If his heart is very big, let him go deep within and see who it is that is suffering in and through the individual. He will see that it is God who is purposely having a special experience in and through that person.

Svadhisthana, the spleen chakra. When one has mastery over svadhisthana, one acquires the power of love. He loves everyone

14

and he is loved by everyone: by men and women and by animals. It is here that people very often fall from the path of Light and Truth. Divine love is expansion and expansion is illumination. Love can be expressed as an expansion of our divine awareness or it can be expressed as pleasure. When the svadhisthana centre is opened, the lower vital, the sex forces will try to lower the consciousness of the seeker. But if at that time he can bring down abundant purity from the anahata centre, the heart centre, then this impurity will be transformed into purity. And purity is eventually transformed into ever-fulfilling and everlasting divinity. But if he cannot bring down purity, then there is real destruction, destruction of the seeker's life. The lower vital acts most vehemently and powerfully and sometimes it becomes worse than the lower vital in ordinary human beings. An ordinary human being does not enjoy the vital life the way some seekers enjoy it after opening their svadhisthana centre.

Manipura, the navel chakra. If one acquires mastery over this centre, one conquers sorrow and suffering. No matter what happens in his life, he will not feel sad or miserable. But this centre can create a problem like the svadhisthana chakra. This centre is also dangerous. One can create suffering for others if one misuses the power from the manipura chakra and he will thereby incur the world's curse. This centre, like the ajna chakra, can show the seeker where a relative or dear one has gone after he dies. It lets one see how the person is passing through the vital world and entering into the subtle world and the higher planes. It shows how he passes from one sheath to another after death. This centre also gives one the power of transmutation. One can magnify an object or one can reduce it to an infinitesimal size. In addition, this centre has healing power. As I said before, if one can use this power properly, in accordance with the Will of God, then it is a real blessing. Otherwise it is a curse.

Anahata, the heart centre. Here the power is unbelievable. A seeker with mastery over the anahata centre has free access to both the visible and the invisible worlds. Time surrenders to him; space surrenders to him. If he uses this centre, he can travel to any part of the world in a few seconds in his subtle body. But if he does this, he takes a great risk. Suppose he wants to travel occultly and spiritually to Europe to see what is happening there. If he does not get the proper sanction from the other centres, or if the other centres do not co-operate, then the other centres may not allow the soul to come back to the body after its journey. In India, I know of quite a few cases where Yogis leave their bodies through the heart centre without taking help or getting permission and without even informing the other centres. They feel that the other centres do not have the same special capacity as the heart centre and so they should use the heart centre. Then the other centres become jealous. Jealousy is everywhere, in the outer world and in the inner world as well. Even the cosmic gods enjoy jealousy. So the other centres, because they are jealous, do not let the soul come back. If one uses this power, one has to take permission from the Inner Pilot first. If the Inner Pilot sanctions it, then the other centres cannot do any harm, since the Inner Pilot has infinitely more power than these centres.

In the anahata centre, one can enjoy the deepest bliss of oneness; one can have pure joy. Any person can look at a flower and get joy, but the intensity of joy that the flower embodies we cannot all enjoy. But if one opens the heart centre and looks at a flower, immediately all the joy, all the beauty that the flower has will become his. If the seeker looks at the vast ocean, inside his heart he is bound to feel the vast ocean. He looks at the vast sky and he enters into the sky, he becomes the sky. Anything vast, pure, divine, sublime that he sees, he can immediately feel as his very own and he can become that thing. There is no yawning gulf between what he sees and what he is. He just becomes in his consciousness what he sees.

This is not his imagination. Far from it! His heart is a divine heart which embodies the universal Consciousness. The spiritual heart is not the heart that we find in our physical body. The spiritual heart is larger than the largest. It is larger than the universal Consciousness itself. We always say that there cannot be anything superior to the universal Consciousness, but this is a mistake. The heart, the spiritual heart, houses the universal Consciousness. This centre is very safe when we use it to identify ourselves with the vast, with the beauty of nature. But when we use it to travel outside the limitations of the body, we take a risk.

Vishuddha, the throat chakra. He who has mastery over vishuddha has the capacity to offer divine messages to the world. Universal nature discloses its agelong hidden mysteries to him. Here nature bows to the seeker. He can retain eternal youth. The outer world surrenders to him. The inner world embraces him. We get messages from various planes of consciousness. But when one gets a message from the vishuddha centre, the message is sublime and everlasting. When this centre is open, one receives direct messages from the Highest and becomes a mouthpiece for the Highest. One becomes a poet, a singer or an artist. All forms of art are expressed from this centre. This centre is open in many individuals. It functions according to the degree to which it is open, according to one's development. There is very little risk in this centre. It is a mild centre; it does not interfere with other centres and the other centres leave it alone.

Ajna, the brow chakra. He who has mastery over the ajna chakra destroys his dark past, hastens the golden future and manifests the present in a supremely fulfilling way. His psychic and occult powers defy all limits; they are endless. The ajna chakra, which is located between and a little above the eyebrows, is the most powerful centre. The first thing one does when his third eye opens, if it is opened properly, is to destroy the unlit, unaspiring and undivine past. Now we see something and we have an experience. But there is a difference between our experience and the thing that we are experiencing. When the ajna centre is opened, however, we experience the thing itself. We become one with the thing that we are experiencing. At that time, seeing and becoming go together. Seeing itself is becoming and becoming is seeing. For this reason, the aspirant who has opened his third eye wants to destroy the past from his memory. In this incarnation suppose one has become a Yogi. When he looks back to his previous incarnation, he sees that he was a thief, or something worse. Since he does not now want to enter into that experience again, he will try to destroy that part of his past. He now has the necessary power.

When one realises God, the past is automatically deleted. As I said before, when one opens the third eye or any other centre, it does not mean that one has realised God. When one realises God, the obscure, impure or undivine past is illumined and nullified all at once. At the moment of God-realisation, illumination takes place. It is like coming out of a dark room into an illumined room. It becomes light where before it was all dark. God-realisation is immediate illumination.

With the ajna chakra, the past can be nullified and the future can be brought into the immediacy of today. If one knows that ten years from now he is going to do something, achieve something or grow into something, then by using the third eye he can achieve that very thing today. He does not have to wait for ten, fifteen, twenty years.

But if one brings the future result to the fore, this can sometimes be dangerous. It has happened many, many times that the future of an individual is very bright, very luminous. But when the future is brought right into the immediacy of the present, the enormity of the result puzzles and frightens the seeker. The seeker is like a young elephant. He is growing in strength and in ten years he will be very powerful. But if the power comes right now, there may be no receptivity, no inner receptivity. The power comes, but it cannot be brought under control or it cannot be contained in a safe vessel. At that time power itself acts like an enemy and destroys the person who invoked it. So there is a great danger when one takes the future and brings it into the present.

Let the present grow and play its role. The past has played its role; now the present wants to play its role. Only in some cases, when God wants a seeker to make very fast progress, instead of going systematically he can run extremely fast. It is just like the situation of a student in school. Sometimes a student does not go through all the grades of kindergarten, primary school and high school. Sometimes he skips grades. In the spiritual life also, if it is God's Will that the future be brought into the present, then there is no danger. But otherwise there is great danger.

With the third eye, one can accomplish much. The third eye *has* what God, the ultimate Power, *is*. If the ultimate Power is misused by the third eye, then it is all destruction. But if the third eye uses the ultimate, transcendental Power properly and divinely, then it will be a great blessing, the greatest blessing that humanity can imagine.

Sahasrara, the crown chakra. The sahasrara is the silent one which does not interfere in anything. It is like the eldest member in the family; it does not bother anyone and does not want to be bothered by anyone. When this centre is opened permanently, one enjoys infinite Bliss and becomes inseparably one with the ever-transcending Beyond. One comes to know that he is birthless and deathless. He is always dealing with Infinity, Eternity and Immortality. These are not vague terms for him; they are all reality. This moment he sees himself as Eternity and he grows into Eternity; the next moment he sees himself as Infinity and he grows into Infinity; a few moments later he sees himself as Immortality and grows into Immortality in his consciousness. And at times it happens that Infinity, Eternity and Immortality all go together in his consciousness.

When the sahasrara chakra is open, the Inner Pilot becomes a true friend. Here the Infinite and His chosen son become very good friends to fulfil a specific mission for their mutual manifestation. They share many secrets, millions of secrets, in the twinkling of an eye. On the one hand Father and son are enjoying infinite Peace and Bliss; on the other hand they are discussing world problems, universal problems, all in the twinkling of an eye. But their problems are not problems as such. Their problems are only experiences in their cosmic game.

Of all the centres, the highest, the most peaceful, the most soulful, the most fruitful is sahasrara. There Infinity, Eternity and Immortality have become one. The Source becomes one with the creation, and the creation becomes one with the Source. Here the knower and the Known, the lover and the Beloved, the slave and the Master, the son and the Father, all become one. Together the Creator and the creation transcend their Dream and Reality. Their Dream makes them feel what they are and their Reality makes them feel what they can do. Reality and Dream become one.

February 21, 1973

CONCENTRATION, MEDITATION, WILLPOWER AND LOVE

Concentration in Kundalini Yoga. A seeker concentrates on the centres to open them. This is a long, arduous, uncertain and dangerous process. If the seeker does not make enough conscious effort, then the process is bound to be long. If the entire being of the seeker does not cooperate, then the process is bound to be arduous. During the journey, if the seeker makes friends with teeming fears, then the process is bound to be uncertain. During the journey, if the seeker makes friends with brooding doubts, then the process is bound to be extremely dangerous.

In all Yogas you need a spiritual teacher. In Kundalini Yoga, the need for a spiritual teacher is paramount. If you follow other Yogas, you undoubtedly need a Master;

but if you do not care for a Master, if you want to go slowly, steadily, like an Indian bullock cart, there is no harm. There is no danger involved in other paths. You will reach your destination only after thousands of years, in another life, but there is no particular danger in your travelling without a guide. But in Kundalini Yoga, if you do not have a real Master to teach you, then you are playing with fire. If the spiritual centres, especially the lower centres — muladhara, svadhisthana and manipura — are opened untimely, without full preparation, they can create untold misery for the seeker. The teacher uses his vast wisdom to shorten the long road for the student. The teacher uses his deep compassion to transform the arduous road into an easy and smooth road for the student. The teacher uses his illumining light to remove uncertainty from the mind of the student and replace it with absolute certainty. The teacher uses his indomitable power to cast aside all danger to the student from the journey's start to the journey's close. He also makes the path a sunlit path, so that the student can run the fastest without danger or obstruction on the way.

Meditation in Kundalini Yoga. The seeker meditates on his mind, on his heart or on any object or subject. But his main aim at the beginning is to empty the mind, still the mind, silence the mind. He meditates to expand his human individuality into God's highest Universality. He meditates to expand his human personality into God's endless and eternal Life. There comes a time in the seeker's life when he discovers that he is at once the lover and the Beloved. The aspiring soul which he embodies is the lover in him. And the transcendental Self which he reveals from within is his Beloved.

In the beginning, in the formative years of his spiritual life, the seeker has to observe some strict disciplines. He has to meditate early every morning at the same hour, in the same place, a place safe from the intrusions of the outer world. If he is fortunate enough, he can face the rising sun while he meditates. The dynamic energy, the creative force, the hope-message of liberation from the rays of the sun will enter into the seeker. Before he enters into meditation, he must take a proper shower so that his outer body will be clean. The seeker should be lightly clad when he meditates, preferably in white, which is the colour of purity. He should burn incense and candles and place flowers in front of him during his meditation to give himself additional inspiration.

In the course of time, if the seeker does all these things, Peace, Light and Bliss will descend on him; and at God's choice Hour he will hear the Voice of Silence. The Voice of Silence will bless the seeker with some intuitive power. If the seeker uses this intuitive power not at his own sweet will, but in accordance with God's Will, gradually he will open the kundalini chakras. This process is quite easy and at the same time the result is quite effective and most satisfactory. The seeker does not go through severe disciplines. He does not concentrate on each centre as other seekers do. He simply uses his intuitive power. Intuitive power can very easily and effectively open the centres for him.

Willpower in Kundalini Yoga. Spiritual Masters of a very high order do not go through concentration and meditation to open their chakras. They simply use their invincible and all-conquering willpower and open the seven centres as easily as a man eats seven grapes. You can call this willpower the light of the soul or the breath of the spirit. This willpower is like divine volcanic power. It does not take them more than a few seconds to open a centre. But these great spiritual Masters also once trod the path of strong concentration and deep meditation. They did not concentrate or meditate on the chakras; they concentrated on God's Feet and meditated on God's Heart. From God's Feet they received God's ceaseless Compassion and from God's Heart they received God's boundless Love. While playing with God's Compassion, they saw and felt that God's Compassion was nothing other than God's indomitable Willpower. While playing with God's Love, they saw and felt that God's Love was nothing other than God's Wisdom-Light.

When these Masters, in the course of time, were granted the use of this boundless Light and Power, they were to use it only when the Inner Pilot commanded and not at their own sweet will. A real spiritual Master has less freedom in the ordinary sense of the term than an ordinary human being. The ordinary human being has a limited power of choice. He can use his limited power of choice to go against God's Will at his own sweet will. But a real spiritual Master has surrendered his individual will to the Will of the Supreme. He can never have any personal will other than the Divine Will.

The Absolute Supreme asks the spiritual Master always to use his Wisdom-Light before using his Willpower. Very often, ordinary Yogis and people who are fond of occultism and magic do not use Wisdom-Light at all. They just use the willpower that comes from the vital. Willpower can come from the vital world or from the soul's region or from the transcendental Self. When we use the Willpower from the transcendental Self, we are safe, totally safe. When we use the willpower from the soul's region, we are also totally safe. But when we use the willpower from the vital— the lower vital, aggressive vital, destructive vital or even the dynamic vital—then we run into danger. Very often people who do this create danger and difficulty for themselves and for others because they do not have proper control of the vital force. But a real spiritual Master first uses God's Wisdom-Light and then uses God's Willpower in order to illumine blind mankind and feed hungry mankind.

Love and the lower vital life in Kundalini Yoga. Real love and the life of the lower vital are two totally different things. Concentration is an outer vigilance. Meditation is an inner vigilance. Concentration says that the life of the lower vital must not be suppressed, but sublimated. Meditation says that the life of the lower vital not only has to be sublimated, but also has to be perfected, illumined and liberated. It is not an easy task to conquer the lower vital movements. It cannot be done all at once, but must be done slowly and steadily. If you run toward the goal at a steady pace, then you are bound to reach it. Always you have to live a life of purity, a life of conscious awareness and a life of self-dedication. Then the lower vital can be transformed into the dynamic, illumined vital, which can be utilised by God Himself.

Concentration tells us that the life of love must not run between the binding human in us and the binding human in others. Concentration further says that the life of love must run between the divine in us and the divine and immortal in God. Only then can our love and God's Love together be fulfilled. Meditation says that the life of love must run between our realisation of God and God's manifestation in us. Meditation further says that the life of love must run between the transformed and perfected passion of the body and the illumining and fulfilling ecstasy of the Spirit.

The animal in us does not know what real love is. The human in us knows perfectly well what real love is, but it feels that real love is beyond its reach. The divine in us knows that real love is within our easy reach. And it tells us soulfully, emphatically and categorically what real love is. Real love is ceaseless self-offering and endless God-becoming.

Most of you know much about concentration and meditation. I wish to say that no matter which path you follow or which Yoga you practise, concentration and meditation have to be given utmost importance. Now what do we mean by concentration? What do we actually do when we concentrate? When you concentrate, you have to feel that nothing exists except the thing that you are concentrating upon. When you concentrate, try to forget the rest of the world: what is within you, around you, before you, above you, below you. Concentrate on only one object. If you want to concentrate on the tip of your thumb, start with imagination. Imagine that your only possession is your thumb. There is nothing else which you can claim as your own. The rest of the body does not belong to you — only the thumb. If you want to concentrate on the tip of your nose, feel that you are the possessor of only your nose; you are not the possessor of your eyes, your ears, your mouth, your limbs. If you begin to think of something else, feel that you are entering into foreign territory. In this way you will develop your power of concentration.

You are at liberty to choose any part of your body to concentrate on, but try to use some part which you feel as your very own. And do not concentrate on your arm or your hand or your leg. Take a very small part of your body, the eye or the nose or the fingertip. The smaller the better for concentration.

If you want to concentrate on your heartbeat, do not be afraid. There are some beginners who feel that when they are concentrating on their heartbeat, their heart will stop and they will die. Tremendous fear enters into them. They feel that they are going to die immediately. They may be able to concentrate on anything else, but when it is a matter of concentrating on the heartbeat, they are terribly afraid. But if you want to be a real hero in your spiritual life, you should try to concentrate on your heartbeat. This is the golden opportunity for you to enter into the endless life. Each time you hear the sound of your heartbeat, immediately feel your infinite, immortal life there.

If you want to develop the power of concentration very rapidly, then please do this. Before you concentrate, wash your face and eyes properly. Then make a black dot on the wall at eye level and stand facing the dot, about ten inches away. Concentrate on the dot. After a few minutes try to feel that while you are breathing in, your breath is actually coming from the dot, and that the dot is also breathing in, getting its breath from you. Try to feel that there are two persons: you and the black dot that you have made. Your breath is coming from that dot and its breath is coming from you. Now in ten minutes' time, if your concentration is very powerful, you will feel that something from within you has left. And what is that something? It is your soul. Your soul has left you and entered into the black dot on the wall. Now feel that you and your soul are conversing. Your soul is taking you into the soul's world for realisation and you are bringing the soul into your world for manifestation. In this way you can develop your power of concentration very easily. But this method has to be practised. There are many things which are very easy with practice, but just because we do not practise we do not get the result.

Always bear in mind that the power of concentration can be developed very rapidly only when you concentrate on a very tiny thing, something as tiny as possible. The power of meditation is totally different, however. When you want to develop the power of meditation, then think of something very vast. Think of the sky or the sea. When you meditate early in the morning or in the evening, you do not have to face the ocean or look up into the sky if you do not want to. Earlier I said that if you can see the rising sun in the morning, it is extremely helpful. But if you do not have the opportunity to see the sun or the sky or the sea, no harm. Try to see the rising sun inside you; try to see the sky inside you; try to see the ocean inside you. Your spiritual heart is infinitely larger than the ocean and infinitely vaster than the sky.

When you meditate, please do not expect anything either from yourself or from God. You will be able to make the fastest progress if you do not expect anything from your meditation. Do not expect that tomorrow you are going to be the b instrument of God or that God will make you His choice instrument tomorrow. Just meditate on God's Heart, which all Light. And if you want to concentrate, concentrate on God's Feet, which are all Compassion. You do not need thousands of things either from your life or from God. You need only God's Compassion and God's Light. If you have these, then you have everything.

Through either concentration or meditation, you can arouse your kundalini. But if you want to develop the kundalini powers, there is an easy process. Practise Hatha Yoga. Here in the West, there are many, many teachers who can teach Hatha Yoga and who are extremely good at doing the exercises. Hatha Yoga will help you to purify your body-consciousness and purity is of great importance in Kundalini Yoga. Hatha Yoga is the union of the sun quality and the moon quality: that is to say, the dynamic quality and the mild quality in us.

The dynamic quality is power and the mild quality is beauty. These two are united in Hatha Yoga. Raja Yoga, on the other hand, is the union of consciousness and illumination. When consciousness and illumination become one, you can achieve anything that you want to achieve.

But if there are some seekers who want only God, God's Light and the highest Truth, then I wish to say that these seekers should follow only one path; and that is the path of self-offering, the path of surrender, the path of constant self-giving. If you want to realise the Infinite, the Absolute, then follow the path of constant and unconditional surrender. If you follow Hatha Yoga, Raja Yoga, Karma Yoga, Bhakti Yoga or Jnana Yoga — no matter which you follow — when you reach your goal it will be like getting a few most delicious mangoes from the tree. You have seen the mangoes and taken them, but the owner is not there. But if you follow the Yoga of unconditional surrender, in which the human will is offered to the divine Will, then you will get the owner of the tree, and the owner will gladly offer you the fruits of all the trees in his garden.

The Yoga of surrender can be practised with and in all other systems of Yoga; but he who wants God alone, God the infinite Truth, God the infinite Peace, infinite Light and infinite Bliss, most assuredly must practise the Yoga of surrender. This surrender is not the surrender of a lazy person. This is the surrender of someone who is dynamic, active and constantly ready to offer himself, to become what God wants him to become.

February 28, 1973

SELF-DISCOVERY
AND
TRANSFORMATION

There are two worlds: the outer world and the inner world. When the kundalini is fast asleep, man is awake to the outer world. He wants to have everything that the outer world can offer him and he feels that he can get satisfaction only from what the outer world can give him.

When the kundalini is awake, man is fully aware of the inner world. He knows that the outer world cannot satisfy his inner needs. He has brought to the fore the capacity of the inner world, which he has come to realise is far superior to the capacity of the outer world. He has brought to the fore the hidden powers, the occult powers, within himself. Either he uses these powers properly or he misuses them. When

he divinely uses the powers of the kundalini, he becomes the real pride of the
Mother Supreme. When he misuses them,
he becomes the worst enemy of man's
embodied consciousness and of his own
personal evolution.

As we all like to play, so also our Divine
Mother and Divine Father like to play. The
Divine Mother, Parvati, and the Divine
Father, Shiva, want to play and they want
their child to participate. But their child is
fast asleep, so they wait for some time.
When they feel that it is high time for him
to get up and they see that there is no sign
that he is about to do so, the Mother most
affectionately gives him a push from below,
from his muladhara chakra, and the Father
affectionately pulls him up from above,
from sahasrara. Then the child gets up.

If the child is in a good, divine consciousness when he gets up, he says, "You
have been waiting for such a long time. I
am so sorry. I beg to be excused. I wish to
play with you. Come, let us start playing
the game." Then the Mother most affectionately teaches the child with Her
dynamic Power how to play the cosmic
Game extremely well. And the Father most
affectionately teaches the child with His

inner illumining Light and Wisdom how to play the Game extremely well. Eventually they make their child a unique and accomplished player. When he becomes an exceptionally good player, he has to fight against three opposing players at the same time. These three formidable opponents are Darkness, Ignorance and Death. To his surprise, he defeats his enemies easily. His is the everlasting victory over these fallen foes.

If the child is in a bad, undivine consciousness when he receives the push and pull from his parents, he says to them, "For God's sake, don't bother me. I need sleep, only sleep. I want nothing else. I do not want to play." Then the parents sadly say, "Sleep, child, sleep. We shall play without you."

Any individual can practise Kundalini Yoga if he sincerely wants to. Or if he only wants to study it, then I must say that Kundalini Yoga is worthy of study with the deepest reverence.

The main objectives of Kundalini Yoga are to realise the dynamic existence in the static existence, to change the lower state of consciousness into the higher state of consciousness, to transform the bondage of the finite into the freedom of the Infinite. The dynamic existence is Shakti and the static existence is Shiva. If Shakti is not present in Shiva, then Shiva will remain static. Shakti, the Mother, is the Power, but it is the Father who houses this infinite Power.

When a seeker wants to identify himself with the Mother-Power, he has to intensify his aspiration. It is through intensity that he becomes one with the Shakti. If he wants to become totally one with the Divine Father, Shiva, it is with sea-like immensity that he can become one with Shiva.

Here in the West there are many who feel that the powers of Kundalini Yoga are nothing but rank superstition. I wish to say that those who cherish this idea are totally mistaken. Even the genuine spiritual Masters have examined Kundalini Yoga and found in their own experiences the undeniable authenticity of its hidden occult powers.

Blessed is he who practises Kundalini Yoga as part of his self-discovery and not in order to acquire power in hypnotism, black magic or other low forms of occultism which operate in and from the vital world. A genuine student of Kundalini Yoga is he who tries to unite the vital power and the spiritual knowledge in perfect harmony with the evolving spirit of life. A genuine seeker never considers the hidden powers or occult powers as his goal. He cares only for God. He longs only for God's loving Presence in his life.

The Kundalini Power is the dynamic power in us. When the dynamic power and the spiritual knowledge go hand in hand, the perfect harmony of the universal Consciousness dawns and the conscious evolution of the human soul reaches the transcendental Self.

There are two ways for one to enter into Kundalini Yoga: through the Tantric process and through the Vedantic process. The Tantric approach is systematic and elaborate but, at the same time, quite dangerous. The Vedantic process is simple and mystical, but it is safe and in no way less convincing or less fulfilling.

The Tantric method is dangerous because it deals first with the lower vital and emotional life. The approach is dynamic and courageous. Either one will purify himself by entering bravely into the vital world and coming out triumphant, or one will be totally lost in the ignorance of the vital world if he is not strong enough inwardly to conquer the vital forces there.

The Vedantic way is safe because the seeker concentrates and meditates to raise, purify and illumine his consciousness before he tries to deal with the obscure, impure lower vital forces that want to bind him. When the seeker enters into the lower vital world with the light of illumination, to his wide surprise he sees that the lower vital is illumined, purified and divinised.

The Tantric process demands from the seeker constant and conscious awareness of the inner and upward movement from the muladhara chakra to the sahasrara chakra. The Vedantic process demands from the seeker conscious and constant awareness of the evolving and liberating consciousness.

If anybody here would like to practise Kundalini Yoga, I advise that seeker to follow the Vedantic method, which is safe and, at the same time, sure. If you follow the Vedantic method, you are destined to reach the Goal certainly and safely.

Stories

Vivekananda showed the sincerity of his inner cry for Truth, for God, for Light. It happened once that Vivekananda, who was then called Naren, was offered a significant gift by his spiritual Master, Sri Ramakrishna. Sri Ramakrishna said to him, "Naren, you know I have gone through the most austere spiritual disciplines. I constantly pray to Mother Kali and worship God. I have done everything necessary and now I am blessed with occult power. But you know that I don't care for any outer achievements. I pay no attention even to wearing clothes. I am in my own world most of the time. So I wish to tell Mother Kali that I would like to offer you all my occult power. You will be able to use it when you have to work for the world at large."

Naren immediately replied, "Master, please tell me whether this power will be of any help to me in my God realisation."

Sri Ramakrishna said, "No, no! You know that occult power has nothing to do with God-realisation. But when you realise God, if you want to work for a while, if you want to manifest God on earth, then this power can be of great help to you."

Naren's immediate response was, "First things first. First I want to realise God. Then if you and God want to give me occult power to use for mankind, I will take it. But right now I want only God. God comes first in my life."

Ramakrishna was extremely pleased with his dearest disciple. He said to the other disciples, "Look at my Naren. Look at the example he has set for you. You have to pay all attention to God first, only to God. That is the only way you can realise God. Occult power is of very secondary importance."

Most genuine spiritual Masters have advised their disciples not to care for the hidden powers of the kundalini. If a disciple cares only for Truth, only for Light, then he will make real progress in his inner life.

We practise Kundalini Yoga in order to get power of one kind or another. But if we meditate on God and please God, the Creator, He will give us His entire creation if He wants to. If we want the Creator first and foremost, and not His creation, then we will get the Creator. And once we have the Creator, His entire creation will also be at our disposal. If we cry for one tiny part of the creation, we may get it with comparative ease; but the infinite Wealth of the Creator will be withheld from us and

we will have to be satisfied with the tiny
portion which we asked for.

*

There is a famous story in India about
two brothers. The elder brother left home
and prayed in the forest most intensely. At
the end of twelve years he returned home.

The younger brother was delighted to see
him and he requested, "Please, please show
me some occult power. You have practised
Yoga for twelve long years while I have
been leading an ordinary life. Please show
me what you have accomplished."

The elder brother said, "Come with me."
The two brothers entered the village and
walked to the river. At the river bank the
elder brother sat down and entered into
deep meditation. After a while he stood up
and walked across the river on the surface
of the water.

Immediately the younger brother hailed
the ferryman, gave him an anna and was
quickly rowed across the river to join his
brother. When the two brothers were
united again, the younger brother said,
"You had to slave for twelve years to be
able to do something that I can do in five

minutes? Is this the result of your years of
spiritual discipline and austere life? Shame,
shame!"

The elder brother realised that he had
foolishly wasted his twelve years. He left
home once more, this time to aspire only
for Truth, only for Light, only for God.

*

When we cry for Truth and Light we get
them, but our cry must be extremely
sincere, devoted and soulful. If we are not
sincere, if we are not pure, if we are not
spiritual, then the Kundalini Power is of no
use. Here is another authentic story.

When I was only nine and a half years
old, on my way back from school one day I
saw a big crowd. Naturally, I went to see
what was happening. One of the spectators
told me that a young man who had been
buried for three days was about to emerge
from the grave. To my astonishment, a few
minutes later the young man did emerge,
quite safe. But then what did he do? As
soon as he came out from the ground, he
put his arm around his girlfriend and
walked away. His vital life went on
unabated.

From Kundalini Yoga he had received the power to remain underground for many days. But what good did it do him? He did not care to purify his vital life. He led a most ordinary life, an animal life. This power did not inspire him or anyone else to lead a better life. He used it only for miracle-mongering. But if the kundalini is used properly, it can do something most significant. It can elevate the consciousness of humanity. Kundalini Power has the capacity to awaken and illumine the consciousness of mankind if it is properly used.

*

There are high occultists and low occultists. The inferior ones fight for occult power in the vital world. As in the outer world unillumined people fight for power, so in the inner world, in the vital world, unillumined occultists also fight for power. If one occultist is fast asleep, another may come and attack him occultly and try to take away his occult power. This once happened to a maternal uncle of mine. Fortunately, my maternal uncle was stronger than the occultist who attacked him and he defeated the other occultist.

But the superior occultists, the spiritual ones, will never do that. And if the spiritual Masters, the real Yogis, have occult powers, they do not try to attack or defeat other spiritual Masters to win more occult power. But spiritual Masters sometimes do take away occult power from unwise seekers. Sometimes they see that a seeker is basically sincere, but he has attained a little occult power and is misusing it. Then out of their infinite compassion, the Masters may take away the occult power of these unfortunate seekers so that they will return to the spiritual life and realise the highest Truth. When the time comes and the seekers are ready to use their occult power wisely, the Masters give it all back.

On at least one occasion, Sri Ramakrishna took away occult power from one or two individuals at the express command of Mother Kali. Sri Ramakrishna himself had occult power in boundless measure and he did not need their occult power. He took away their power for the seekers' own spiritual good. These seekers were basically sincere. They had the capacity to cry for the highest Truth, but they were being distracted by their occult power and were not paying attention to their real spiritual life.

In the case of another spiritual Master, he and his younger brother started Yoga almost at the same time. But when the elder brother accepted a shakti to help him in his spiritual work, the younger brother left him and started an ashram of his own. He also had a little occult power, but he started misusing it, so the elder brother took it away. The younger brother then wrote pathetic letters to his elder brother, saying, "I know you have infinitely more occult power than I had. Why did you take away the little occult power I had?" But the elder brother replied, "It is for your own good. You have left me, but I have boundless concern for your spiritual life. I want you to realise the Highest. I don't want you to waste your time showing off your occult power and in that way to lose all your spirituality and divine possibilities."

Let me tell you a story about misuse of occult powers. About one hundred and fifty years ago there was a spiritual Master named Matsyendranath. His dearest disciple's name was Gorakshanath. When Matsyendranath realised that Gorakshanath would also become spiritually great, he told him, "Look, two lions cannot live in the same area. We should not stay together now. You should go somewhere else to roam. You have the capacity. You should now guide the world, as I am guiding it."

Gorakshanath felt miserable, but he had to listen to his Master's command. So he left Matsyendranath and stayed away for six years. At the end of six years he returned to the place where he had parted from his Master. When he got there, he asked his brother disciples and the people who were in the neighbourhood if they knew where his Master was. They all said, "We can't tell you where the Master is."

Gorakshanath pleaded with them, saying that he had not seen his Master for six years and that he was Matsyendranath's dearest disciple, but they all said, "No! You are not his dearest disciple. You are just making yourself important. And if you *are* his dearest disciple, then you should listen to his command. He told us that nobody should be allowed to know where he is." And they refused to tell Gorakshanath where his Master was.

Finally Gorakshanath became furious. He said, "Now I shall curse you. For twelve years you will have no rain at all. That means no crops, no food, no drinking water. All of you will die of starvation if you stay here. Only on the condition that my Master comes back here will this curse be lifted before the end of twelve years."

The drought began immediately. When conditions became serious, the King of that particular area went to Gorakshanath and pleaded with him to lift his curse, but Gorakshanath refused. The drought continued for two and a half years. When word of Gorakshanath's curse finally reached Matsyendranath, he went back to the area immediately. Then it began to rain. Matsyendranath stood in front of Gorakshanath and said, "I am so happy to see you again."

Gorakshanath immediately recognised his stupidity. "Forgive me, Master," he said. "I am ashamed of what I have done to these people."

But Matsyendranath said to his favourite disciple, "You have not done anything wrong. These people were all corrupt. They deserved this kind of punishment. It will help them lead a better life."

Gorakshanath said, "But I did not know that. I merely wanted to punish them. I was angry. My action was bad because my motive was bad."

"I am not offering any false justification," said Matsyendranath. "Your soul knew that they deserved punishment. What you have done is right."

When the Master uses his compassion-power, he uses it to protect his disciples as well as to correct their misdeeds. The Master ultimately wants perfection from his disciples. Compassion is the means. Perfection is the end.

*

The same Master and the same disciple had another significant experience. Gorakshanath had tremendous pride because he had realised the Truth and attained occult power, so Matsyendranath wanted to show him that using occult power can be extremely dangerous. Here is the story of that incident.

A Yogi once came to Gorakshanath and started insulting him and his Master, Matsyendranath. Gorakshanath said, "Don't you dare speak about my Master that way! I have tremendous occult power."

The Yogi challenged him, "Show me your occult power!"

"Here is a knife. If you strike me any-where on my body you will not be able to injure me at all. This is my power."

The Yogi started stabbing Gorakshanath, but not even a hair of his body was de-stroyed. Then the Yogi said to him, "All right. Whenever I struck you there was al-ways a sound. Although you were not in-jured, my blows created a sound. But if you strike me with the same knife, not only will you not be able to injure me, but also you will not be able to produce any sound."

Gorakshanath started striking the Yogi with the knife and the Yogi's claim proved true. There was not even any sound. The Yogi then said to Gorakshanath, "If one identifies with the Infinite, then no sound will be produced by a blow. This proves that I am superior to you in occult power." Pleased with his victory, the Yogi walked away.

Matsyendranath was somewhere else when all this occurred, but Gorakshanath concentrated deeply on him in order to speak to him about this experience. His vision told him that Matsyendranath was in an ashram in Mayapuri, Illusion City. To his wide surprise he saw his Master sur-rounded by many beautiful girls. They were dancing around him and he was enjoying vital life, emotional life. Gorakshanath said to himself, "How can it be? My Master is of the highest order. Perhaps my vision is wrong." Again Gorakshanath concentrated and he saw the same scene. This time he was positive that his Master was there. "My Master has fallen!" he thought. "He is surrounded by so many beautiful girls, all singing and dancing. He is enjoying all kinds of vital life. I must save him."

So Gorakshanath opened his heart centre and transported himself to the ashram in Mayapuri occultly. At the gate he asked about his Guru. The gatekeeper said, "Matsyendranath? Your Guru? He has fallen. What he was and what he has become now! He has fallen to such an extent that I cannot believe it."

Gorakshanath immediately wanted to go and rescue his Guru, but the women would not allow him to approach Matsyendranath. Gorakshanath had to use his occult power to become a beautiful woman and join in the dancing and singing. When he came near Matsyendranath in the guise of a dancing girl, Matsyendranath could not recognise his disciple. Then Gorakshanath had to use his occult power to speak to his Master.

"Master, what are you doing here?" he cried. "What kind of life are you leading? You are a God-realised soul. What are you doing here enjoying vital life?"

Matsyendranath immediately said, "Oh, I am fallen. I am fallen to such an extent! Now save me." So Gorakshanath used his occult power and took Matsyendranath away from Mayapuri. When they had gone six or seven miles away, Matsyendranath came out of maya, illusion, and he was free. The disciple and the Master travelled two thousand miles until they came to Matsyendranath's ashram in North India. There Gorakshanath saw that Matsyendranath had two spiritual bodies. One body had flown with him through occult power, and the other was just before him at the destination. In a few minutes the Master who had flown with him entered into the other Master who was facing him. And suddenly Gorakshanath saw that many of his Master's disciples were around him. He asked one disciple, "Has Master been away for a few years?"

"No," replied the disciple. "For the last few years Master has been here and we have all been with him."

Then Gorakshanath said, "How can this be? Master, please explain this experience I have just gone through. I cannot fathom the mystery of what has actually happened."

Matsyendranath replied, "I had to do all that just for you. You had all kinds of occult power, but your pride was too great. You were very austere and rigid in your spiritual life. You looked down on women. I told you repeatedly that by looking down on women you would not be able to perfect and transform your life. You did not care for women's liberation from ignorance. You felt that women are an open door to hell and that it is they who create all problems, especially vital problems, in men's lives. But this is not true. It is men's own imperfections that create problems. Men have weaknesses; and when they project these weaknesses onto women, they feel that women are the cause of all their problems. Both men and women are God's creations and they both have to conquer the lower vital movements. Right from the beginning I have been telling you that women must not be shunned. They have to be helped, freed from the mire of ignorance.

"You are my best disciple. I gave you all kinds of occult power, but you were defeated by that Yogi, only because of your pride. Now that you have been humiliated, now that your pride has been smashed, I wish to tell you something. Although you are my student and although you lost to that Yogi, before long you will surpass both him and me. You are my student today, but tomorrow perhaps I shall be your student. Because today you have conquered your pride, because today you are seeing the Truth in a divine way, your tremendous potentiality will now be able to come to the fore. You are bound to surpass us. Also, when you became a woman in order to approach me, in order to help me, you learned not to shun women. You came to realise that men and women must go together toward the transcendental Goal. Now that you have learned this truth from me, there is nothing else that I can teach you. All that I have, I have given to you; and by the Grace of the Lord Supreme you have surpassed me." Then Matsyendranath folded his hands and bowed to his disciple.

*

Kundalini Yoga is the Yoga of Shakti, the power of the divine Goddess. We have to value the Mother aspect and see the

59

spiritual Mother in each woman. There was a time when people used to say that women were not meant for spiritual life. Those days are now gone. Now it is clear that men and women aspire equally well. Woman can never be a hindrance to man's progress provided man gives due value to woman's aspiration. Woman's aspiration and dedication can go perfectly well with man's aspiration and dedication. In Kundalini Yoga it is the Mother, the Divine Mother, who fulfils and liberates. When the Divine Mother liberates man and woman from the meshes of ignorance, she feels that her role is over. Kundalini is the power of Shakti and each woman represents the transcendental Shakti, the Mother-Power.

It is through our soulful surrender to the Supreme Mother in us, the Kundalini, that we can liberate our earthly existence and be freed from ignorance. It is through our constant surrender to the Will of the Supreme Mother in us that we can fulfil ourselves.

To each of you I offer my deepest gratitude. You have come here with utmost sincerity to learn about the Mother-Power. Nothing gives me greater joy than to be of service to all your aspiring souls. Some of you are following the path of Kundalini

Yoga; some of you are following other paths. There are various roads to follow, but they all lead us to the same ultimate Goal. What we need is sincerity. What we need is purity. What we need is a conscious and constant inner cry. Then the Goal, the transcendental Goal, will be within our easy reach.

March 7, 1973

MOTHER, IF I LOSE TO YOU

Mother, if I lose to You,
That is my only Victory.
Whatever I have given into Your Hands,
Is only my savings.
To me the rest is of no value,
A mere waste,
And it only tortures me and
Stands as a burden on my way.
I cannot put it to use.
When I lose to You,
After I have achieved
My full realisation,
I know my greatest reward I shall receive.

During his numerous public meditations and university lectures over the past several years, Sri Chinmoy has been asked hundreds of questions about Kundalini Yoga. A selection of some of the more interesting of these, with Sri Chinmoy's answers, follows.

HOW LONG?

How long more shall I cry, Mother?
How long shall I cry
In a dark room alone, loving You?
You know my secret thoughts.
You know my heart's eagerness.
Why does dark death torture me every day?
How long will You delay, Mother?
How long will You delay?
As Jesus had Mary,
So are You my World-Mother.

Question: Where are the chakras located? Are they in the body?

Sri Chinmoy: When we think of the chakras, we think of them as being inside something—that is, inside the subtle body. Sthula sharira is the gross physical. Inside this body is the sukshma sharira, the subtle body. And inside the subtle body is karana sharira, the causal body. These bodies are totally different, but they are all members of the same family. The subtle body at times operates through the physical. At times the causal body, which is in seed form, can operate in and through the subtle body and the physical body. Although the causal body is like a tiny seed, from this seed a banyan tree can grow. It takes a few years, but then the banyan tree bears thousands of fruits. The potentiality of the seed is infinite.

Now, the chakras are not only in the subtle physical; they are also in the universe. According to some Masters, the spiritual heart is the universe; they have gone so far as to say that the universe is inside the heart. Nothing is beyond or outside the spiritual heart.

Question: Are there specific mantras we can use to open up the different centres?

Sri Chinmoy: Yes, inside each centre is a particular deity and we can invoke this deity by chanting his seed-sound. Each sound represents a different state of consciousness. At the base of the spine there is the muladhara chakra. For this centre, the seed-sound is *Lam*. If you can repeat *Lam* while focusing your attention at the base of your spine, in the course of time you will be endowed with occult powers. A few inches higher there is the svadhisthana chakra. For this centre you can repeat the mantra *Vam*. This is a most powerful mantra. Then, at the navel, manipura, you can concentrate and repeat the word *Ram*. If you do it properly, you will see spiritual fire all around you. Next comes the heart. Here you can repeat *Yam*. Although for the previous mantras you could chant powerfully and forcefully, this mantra has to be chanted slowly and sweetly. However, if you want to concentrate on your heart but do not wish to follow the path of Kundalini Yoga, you can chant *Supreme*. Then we come to the throat centre, vishuddha. If you chant *Ham*, you will get the power of eloquence and expression. Finally we come to the ajna chakra. Here the seed word is *Aum*. No matter which mantra you repeat, you have to feel that a current is flowing through your spinal cord and that all the centres are being ecstatically vibrated.

Question: When a centre opens up, will it give any kind of signal?

Sri Chinmoy: Yes, it will give a signal, although people often don't notice it. It will start off like a quarter circle and then go to a full circle. When it begins to turn very, very rapidly, it means that that particular centre is ready to be opened. It is like a wheel that goes on spinning. Then, when the centre is opened up, one gets the experience of feeling the kundalini power rise. Some seekers say that it coils up like a snake; for others it appears to crawl like an ant or jump like a frog.

There is no hard and fast rule that the seeker will get a certain kind of experience. One can expect anything. If the chakras are open, immediately you will be able to know. It is just like opening a door. The door is closed now, bolted from the inside or outside. But once it is open you will be able to know what is inside the room. If the door to your third eye is opened, then you will be able to see the past, present and future. You will have the power of clairvoyance. More than that, you will see that in clairvoyance you will also have the power of clairaudience. You are seeing me here; but if something is going on over there, you will have the power to hear it. But if your heart centre is not opened, you will not have the power to hear the soundless sound in the heart. When your heart centre is opened, you will automatically have the feeling of universal oneness. You touch something and immediately you will identify with it and feel your oneness. You will look at a person and feel oneness with his suffering or joy or any condition he is in. When a particular centre is opened, the qualities of that centre you will get. So if a centre is open, naturally you will feel it. But sometimes people read books and try to meditate and then they immediately feel that their centres are open. This is sheer imagination. It is not an easy thing to open up the centres; it takes very, very serious practice.

Question: What happens if we open the centres before the system has been purified?

Sri Chinmoy: If one opens up the chakras without purification of the vital, especially the lower vital, then one can become unbalanced, mad, insane. Many people go crazy when they open up the chakras before purification takes place. Awakening the kundalini power without first being purified is like giving a child a knife. There is every possibility of his misusing it. He may cut his finger or do something most harmful and damaging. But if one is grown up and mature, then he will use the knife to cut fruit and offer it to his friends.

Power can be utilised in two ways: either to build or to break. We have come here to build, to build the Palace of Truth and Love. Now, while building, we have to know if we are an expert architect or builder. If we are not, then the building will not be perfect and at any moment it will collapse.

So we have to know when it is advisable for us to awaken the kundalini power. When we feel that our inner vessel is pure, when it can receive Light without any obstruction, then we can easily open up the chakras without any danger. But if we arouse the kundalini untimely through our persistent desire and effort, then we may run into great difficulty.

If you wish to follow the path of kundalini, my humble advice to you is to first try to awaken the heart centre. The heart centre is considerably pure. The vital or disturbing emotions will be purified by the opening of this centre. If you can first open up the heart centre and from there take the purity and enter into the lower centres, then there is no danger.

Question: When one enters into the spiritual life, does the kundalini automatically arise, or does this happen only in certain people?

Sri Chinmoy: There are various paths that lead to the Goal. Kundalini is one path that offers special power, but there are other paths which also offer similar powers. Let us say there are three roads leading toward the same destination. One road has quite a few trees and flowers, the second has a few trees and flowers and the third one does not have any at all. While walking the kundalini path, you see some power, but this power is definitely not the ultimate power. For those who have no spiritual or occult power, kundalini power seems very vast. But in comparison to the power of the Goal, kundalini power is nothing.

On some paths, this kind of occult power is not there. The road is clear and you just go forward and reach the Goal. Then, once you reach the Goal, you get the omnipotent power, spiritual power. But the follower of kundalini often just stays with his limited power. On very rare occasions seekers have fallen from the spiritual path because they have achieved spiritual power. Kundalini power, occult power, has taken many, many sincere seekers away from the Truth.

Most of the time, kundalini power is a curse and not a blessing. If you misuse kundalini power, then you are ruined. You destroy all your possibilities to realise the Highest and God knows how many incarnations it will take you to come back to the right path again. Ninety-nine percent of the time the kundalini power is misused. But if you properly use it, then you get inspiration to do something good for the world.

There are many spiritual Masters of the highest order who do not have kundalini power because they have not followed that path, but they have spiritual power, which is much stronger. The real power, spiritual power, comes to the seeker in the process of his inner growth.

Again, if God is pleased with a seeker who is following a different path, He can give the seeker a little bit of kundalini power. If He feels that the seeker may need kundalini power in the future in order to manifest Him in a specific way, then God sends some messenger who is working in kundalini to give that person power. All the different spiritual qualities are in God's room. If you enter into God's room, here you will see one box marked Peace, and other boxes marked Light, Love, Delight and Power. Now you are only caring for Peace, but God feels that you may also need a little bit of Power. The world is such that if you don't show a little bit of power, people don't believe. So if God feels the necessity for Power in your life, even though you don't want kundalini power, God will give it. But if God does not feel any necessity, then even if you cry for kundalini power, He will not give it to you.

People start their spiritual journey with a good attitude; they care only for God, Truth, Light. But after walking for two or three or six months, they find that the path is very dry. They see that they are not getting name and fame or that they are not getting any miraculous power; so they give up and follow another path like kundalini. On that path, as soon as you get something, you can show all your miraculous power to the world and feel that you are something. But this power will never give you even an iota of peace of mind.

The use of occult power in no way elevates anybody's consciousness. Like a magician, you are showing something and it creates a kind of excitement that lasts for a few minutes or an hour. But then you and those who have become excited feel miserable. You know that this is not going to last forever, that there are higher truths and higher realities. You say, "I came into the world for peace, for love, for joy, for happiness, for satisfaction. Now is this the satisfaction that I want?" So you enter into the real spiritual life, where kundalini is not required. Here what is required is only an inner cry for Truth, Light and Bliss. Once you get Truth, Light and Bliss you won't care for kundalini power.

It is just like a child who has five cents. He knows that he will be able to distribute those five cents to five children of his age. But when the child knows that his father has thousands of dollars, then he will not be interested in the five cents. So here, the thousands of dollars is the real spiritual power.

If you want to be satisfied with a little bit of kundalini power, meditate for a few hours daily for six or seven years, which is nothing. In order to realise God it takes quite a few incarnations, unless you have a good spiritual Master. If you *only* concentrate on the chakras and meditate for kundalini, then as you complete your school course in fourteen or fifteen years, so also you will easily get kundalini power. And, if you are a very good student, you can skip a few grades and get kundalini power in just four or five or six years.

Question: Is the awakening of the kundalini a sign that God-realisation is imminent? At what stage of the soul's evolution does the kundalini rise?

Sri Chinmoy: There is no hard and fast rule. There are many people who have realised God without ever having developed kundalini power. It is not at all necessary to open up the centres in order to realise God. They have seen the gradual development, revelation and manifestation of the soul's potentialities and possibilities but have not developed their kundalini power. Here, soul's manifestation means soul's evolution. Again, there are those who will not realise God for another two or three incarnations who have developed kundalini power. So there is no direct connection between the kundalini power and the soul's development.

The opening of the centres need not be an indication of God-realisation. But when there is intense meditation, very powerful meditation of the highest type, then automatically the centres open up. Also, when one realises God, everything comes. At that time the centres automatically open, whether the seeker wants to utilise them or not.

Question: So the awakening of the kundalini does not mean that one is realising God?

Sri Chinmoy: When one's kundalini is awakened, one becomes conscious of his inner psychic power, but this does not mean he is realising God. God-realisation is infinitely superior to the awakening of the kundalini and infinitely more fulfilling. When one's kundalini is awakened, one feels the inner vibration and inner power at his command. But this inner power does not mean the infinite Peace, Light and Bliss of the Supreme.

When the kundalini is awakened, it is like having a penknife with which one can do various things. But when one realises God, one feels that he has the capacity to use the atom bomb. When one realises God, his divine consciousness bursts into the earth's atmosphere and spreads over all the length and breadth of the world. But when the kundalini is awakened, one has only limited power. After the awakening of the kundalini, one sees the limitation of kundalini power. Then one wants to go high, higher, highest and naturally one will march on until the infinite Goal is realised.

Question: If it is not necessary for the kundalini to awaken, why does it awaken in some Masters?

Sri Chinmoy: When somebody is a spiritual Master, the Supreme may want to give him an experience. The Master has to know that something does exist, even though he may not use it. Otherwise, somebody will ask him, "Do you know the kundalini?" Then, if he has not experienced it, the Master will say, "No, it does not exist."

Question: Does sexual indulgence prevent one from acquiring occult power through Kundalini Yoga?

Sri Chinmoy: Kundalini Yoga is the Yoga of absolute purity. It is one of the most sacred Yogas and physical, vital, mental and psychic purity is of paramount importance. The three major nerves—ida, pingala and sushumna—will suffer immensely and immediately if there is any sexual indulgence. And it is not only physical relations that are bad. If somebody enjoys lower vital thoughts, impure thoughts, in the mind, that is also harmful. There are many who have concentrated on the centres and who were about to open them when unfortunately they entered into the lower vital world.

There are many Indian spiritual seekers who have said that when the kundalini is awakened, the vital heat, dynamic heat inside the subtle body very often causes them great discomfort. This energy comes from the subtle body, but it is felt in the physical body. Very often seekers who are about to develop spiritual powers find that the intense inner power is too difficult to bear. So they enter into the ordinary lower vital world and lose the kundalini experience.

To have the kundalini experience for a minute or two or for a few days is not difficult. The most difficult thing is to open up the centres. But this is not the end of our journey. Opening up the centres will give us psychic power or occult power or spiritual power. But the most important thing is to live in the Divine Consciousness.

If one really wants to learn occultism, two things have to be totally shunned. I am talking of strict occultism, not black magic and all that, which anyone can practise. The two things to be shunned are fear and sex. If there is any fear, either in the physical or in the mental or in the psychic, then the great dynamic occult powers can never be developed. And if there are lower vital movements, sex indulgence and impure thoughts in the being, then no occult power can enter.

Question: Are there only seven centres?

Sri Chinmoy: No, there are more. Below the navel, below the spine, there are other centres. There are centres in the subconscient or inconscient planes in the knee, the ankle, the instep of the foot, the toes. When these centres are opened up, one gets full mastery over his physical nature and it becomes quite easy to bring about the total transformation of his earthly life.

Question: Where is the third eye located?

Sri Chinmoy: The ajna centre or third eye is located right between and slightly above the eyebrows, in the centre of the forehead. In the beginning, if you find it difficult to locate, please look in a mirror and place a dot in the centre of your forehead, a little above the eyebrows. In this way you can fix the place.

Question: How does one open the third eye?

Sri Chinmoy: There are various ways to open the third eye. The easiest and most effective way to open the third eye is through japa. Japa means the recitation of a particular syllable, word, sentence or group of sentences. There are quite a few mantras that also help in opening the third eye. The Gayatri Mantra, for example, helps in opening the third eye, for it invokes the infinite knowledge, wisdom and light. Most effective is the chant *Aum.* Each centre has a secret sound which is most effective. For the third eye, the ajna centre, the chant *Aum* is most effective. The 'm' sound should last about three times as long as the 'au' sound. Also, when chanting, the seeker should focus his attention on the third eye.

The third eye can also be opened up by another process, by invoking the presence of the Divine, the consciousness of the Divine or the Divine Consciousness. The Divine may take form or it can remain formless. But you need intense aspiration.

There is a third method: purification of the entire being. Also, inside the body there is the subtle body, the vital proper, the subtle vital, the mind and the heart. If you can achieve the purification of your entire physical and inner existence and get inner illumination, then you can open not only your third eye but all the other major centres as well.

Again, if you can invoke the infinite Grace of the Supreme, if you can transform your whole existence into a living surrender at the Feet of the Supreme, then the third eye can easily be opened. On your part you have to work; your spiritual teacher will give you special exercises and special disciplines to follow. But the result comes only when the Grace descends. Personal effort is indispensable, but mere personal effort is not enough. Behind personal effort is the Grace of the Divine.

Grace can come from God directly or it can come through a living Master or from a Master who has left the body. A realised Master never dies; he only discards the physical garment. Realised Masters can come at any moment to inspire the seeker and tell him what to do. In the case of an ordinary human being, it is "Out of sight, out of mind." But with realised souls, time and space do not matter. Nor do they matter to a seeker if he has an inner connection with a true spiritual Master.

Question: Is there a particular centre I can meditate on in order to control my thoughts?

Sri Chinmoy: Now if you want to control your thoughts, you should concentrate on the centre between the eyebrows. If you become very stiff and your concentration is intense, then you should not concentrate here for more than two minutes. Otherwise, you will become exhausted in the beginning.

Now, if you concentrate on the heart centre, you will get peace, love and joy. Try to hear the cosmic sound, the soundless sound, when you enter into the heart. If you bring love, joy, peace and bliss up from the heart to the centre between the eyebrows, then you will see that there will be no thoughts.

The heart is the safest place for you to concentrate and meditate on. If you do this, automatically you will get purification, because inside the heart is the soul and the soul is one with the Infinite. It is from here that you will get everything.

Question: Is the third eye the best place to focus one's attention during meditation, or can this lead to problems?

Sri Chinmoy: In the spiritual life, you should pray to God to grant you the inner sight only when He feels that it is necessary, not before. If the inner sight dawns when there is not sufficient wisdom, there can be serious problems. It is like having a horse which you cannot keep under control. Let me give you an example. Suppose you see somebody killing a chicken right in front of you. Your outer sight does not let you identify yourself with the consciousness or life-breath of the chicken. But if you have the inner sight and realise that you yourself were a chicken many, many incarnations ago, you will immediately identify yourself with the chicken and feel that you are being killed. You will be horror-struck. When the inner vision dawns, you become one with the reality that you see. And if it is a frightening experience, for years you may suffer. Many of you say, "Oh, if only I had my third eye open!" Yes, and if your third eye shows you that in your past incarnation you were the worst possible scoundrel, then what will you do? The inner sight should be open when there is inner maturity and when neither the past nor the future will disturb you.

Suppose you learn that your dearest friend is going to die, or that some catastrophe is going to take place which you are helpless to prevent. The third eye can tell you what is going to happen, but the third eye cannot prevent it. It is only aspiration, inner cry, that climbs up to the Highest and touches the Feet of the Supreme; and it is only the Supreme who can nullify the cosmic Law. If you see that a catastrophe is going to take place, you have to refer the matter to the Supreme. But if it is God's Will, you cannot prevent it from happening. Now, when a real seeker, a great spiritual seeker sees that something is going to happen to his immediate family — that someone is going to die, let us say — then immediately he will identify Himself with God's Will. But only a real seeker who is on a very high level of aspiration can consciously and spontaneously identify himself with God's Will without any difficulty. Real spiritual Masters are always one with the Supreme's Will; they can never have any individual will of their own. They may feel sorry when they see that something is going to happen, but their inner being remains undisturbed.

So in the case of a spiritual Master or someone who is on the verge of realisation, if his third eye is open he will not be in difficulty. But for an ordinary seeker who has just launched into the spiritual path, if he attempts to open his third eye when his nature is not purified and there is not much spiritual development, then there will be great danger. Many times the vessel is not ready, but by dint of the seeker's tremendous determination, he does succeed in opening up the third eye. Then the result is most discouraging and most damaging.

In your case, instead of opening the third eye, you should meditate on the heart and try to feel God's presence there all the time. You have to want only to be inside God's Heart and to keep Him inside your heart. Then God will make you into His own image and give you only what is best for you. He won't give you an iota of anything unnecessary in your life. Try to draw into your inner being Peace, Joy and Love from God. If you enter into the heart, you will be able to enter into your own inner sun. If you enter properly, you will see that it is all luminosity; no ignorance can stand in front of the inner sun. Immediately this sun either illumines or transforms our ignorance-night. So if you want to realise the Highest and fulfil the Highest in your life, then try to aspire in the heart.

So if you are meditating on the ajna chakra or third eye, you should also practise concentrating on the heart. You will get all joy and all love in the heart, far beyond your expectation. Here you will become inseparably one with the Universal Consciousness. When you have achieved joy and love and have become well-established in your meditation, then you may want to have vision or wisdom from the third eye. There are people who have opened up this centre between the eyebrows without having opened their heart centre and, by the Grace of the Supreme, have not made so-called mistakes. But most of the time, unless and until the heart centre, anahata, is opened up and the emotional part of your nature is totally purified, you will fall victim to merciless temptation if you open up the third eye. You will try to see something inwardly and immediately you will tell people, or you will try to enter into somebody to see what is happening in his nature. There are a thousand and one things which will eventually lead you far, far away from the path of spirituality.

Women, without exception, should try to meditate on the heart centre, the anahata chakra. It is easier for them to open the heart centre than it is for men. For men, it is easier to open up the ajna chakra or the third eye. But both men and women must open both centres eventually. There are other centres as well, but let us think of these two centres for now. While meditating, concentrate on the heart centre first, and then on the ajna.

Question: When the third eye is open, what can you do?

Sri Chinmoy: The third eye is the place of vision. When you use your two eyes, you can see only what is in front of you. But with the third eye you can see forward, backward, everywhere. You can also see the past, present and future at the same time. Right now you may not remember what you ate yesterday for breakfast. But if you can open up your third eye, you will be able to tell even two years ago what you ate for breakfast. If you open your third eye, immediately it will take you into your past, where everything is recorded. It will also show you the future: what is going to happen in your life or in your friends' lives. Suppose you have planned to do something tomorrow morning. This is your plan, your determination. When the day dawns, however, you may change your mind twenty times. But if you see with your third eye what is going to happen, then you will have no necessity, no will to change the cosmic Plan, for it is already done on the inner plane.

Question: What is the relationship between the third eye and the heart centre?

Sri Chinmoy: Let us say that the heart is Consciousness and the third eye is Light, although there is no actual difference between the two. The third eye or ajna chakra can annul or destroy the previous karma, it can expedite the present evolution and it can bring to the fore the future wealth. The third eye has infinite Light and at the same time *is* infinite Light; and the heart or anahata chakra possesses infinite Consciousness and at the same time *is* infinite Consciousness. These two are eternal friends. This moment the infinite Light—which I am calling the third eye—is a building; and inside it is the heart, which is the resident. But the moment the infinite Consciousness—which I am calling the heart—can become the building, the third eye will become the resident. Like this they constantly change.

Although Consciousness and Light are inseparable, some spiritual Masters have seen Light before Consciousness and others have seen Consciousness before Light. The one which they see first, they feel is the Source of the other. It is like this. These two fingers are on the same hand. Suppose the name of this finger is Light and the name of this finger is Consciousness. If you see the one called Light first, then immediately you will say, "The Source is Light." And you will see that Consciousness itself is inside this Light. But if you see the Consciousness-finger first, then you will say, "The Source is Consciousness." And you will see that Light is inside this Consciousness. Some spiritual Masters of the highest order see Consciousness first, while others see Light first. And depending on which they see first, they feel that the Source of everything is either Light or Consciousness.

But a time comes when they see that both Light and Consciousness are inseparable. They go together, like the obverse and reverse of a coin. When I am buying something from you, if I give you a quarter, it does not matter which side is turned toward you. You accept it because you are sure that the other side is there too. Whatever is required is there. So Light and Consciousness always go together. If one does not live in the transcendental Consciousness, the spiritual heart cannot function properly.

Yes, we can separate the two when we use our human knowledge and wisdom. But when we use our divine wisdom, divine light, divine consciousness, we cannot separate the spiritual heart from the third eye. They are complements, like husband and wife. Since the heart usually is all sweetness and love and the third eye is all power and illumination-light, we can say the heart is the wife and the third eye is the husband. The wife's main qualities are softness, kindness, while the husband's main qualities are knowledge, wisdom and other mental things.

But again, those who are very wise feel that the third eye is also the heart, for what else is the heart except that which gives us satisfaction? And what can give us satisfaction? Only Light! So if Light from the third eye gives us satisfaction, then naturally we are dealing with the heart's quality. And what can give us a constant sense of wisdom? Wisdom comes only when we are deep inside the inmost recesses of our breath, inside our heart where Infinity, Eternity and Immortality play. To possess Infinity as our very own, to possess infinite Light and Bliss eternally as our very own: this is wisdom. So we can say that wisdom comes from the heart. Like this the heart and the third eye go together. Like Purusha and Prakriti, God as the Father and God as the Mother, the third eye and the heart go together.

Question: Once when you meditated, I noticed that you touched your third eye first and then your heart centre. What does this mean?

Sri Chinmoy: The third eye is the vision centre. First we want to enjoy the vision of

Bliss. And then, after we have enjoyed the Bliss, we have to put it somewhere for permanent use. And that is the heart.

Question: What is the difference between the ordinary human heart and the spiritual heart or anahata chakra?

Sri Chinmoy: The human heart is a small muscle in the chest which the doctors can show us. But the spiritual heart is something which a seeker sees, feels and grows into. The spiritual heart is vaster than the vastest. Right now, Infinity is an imaginary concept for us. But when we discover our inner heart, our spiritual heart, Infinity is no longer imagination; it is reality.

The universe, the universal Consciousness, the eternal Consciousness, the infinite Consciousness are all inside the spiritual heart. On the one hand, this spiritual heart houses Divinity, Immortality, Eternity and Infinity; on the other hand, it transcends everything.

The spiritual heart is here in the chest, here in the forehead, everywhere. Because it is infinite, it pervades the entire universe.

God is omnipotent, not because He is larger than the largest, but because this moment He can be the tiniest and most insignificant ant and the next moment He can be infinitely vaster than the ocean. Him we call God precisely because He can be whatever He wants to be: vaster than the vastest or tinier than the tiniest. The spiritual heart also has the same capacity. Although it is infinite, eternal and immortal, it can easily reside inside the gross physical heart. Again, it has the capacity to take the physical heart into its Vastness, into its Infinity, into its Eternity.

At one moment the Infinite will separate itself from the finite; at the next moment it will welcome the finite into itself and become totally one with the finite. In the spiritual life, not only can the drop of water enter into the ocean, but the ocean also has the capacity to enter into the tiny drop.

Question: Would you say that the heart centre sometimes opens for a few seconds and then closes again?

Sri Chinmoy: It is true. Sometimes it opens for a few seconds, a few minutes, or a few days; then it may close again. It is like a window. You can leave a window open for a minute, for an hour or for a few days; it is up to you. When aspiration is intense and we become fully one with our soul, this centre remains all the time open. Otherwise, it is open for a minute or a day and then it closes again. But when the six major centres from ajna to muladhara are fully open, then it is very rare that one centre will close.

Question: How do you know that the heart centre is open?

Sri Chinmoy: When the heart centre is open, you will feel boundless joy, boundless love and boundless purity. The first thing you will have is purity: purity inside you, outside you. You will feel infinite love, boundless love, and this love is absolutely pure. It will be within you and without. Then, you will see joy in everything. Now you are crying for joy, but a day will come when this centre is opened and you will get spontaneous joy from everything. You will look at a flower and get joy, you will look at a child and get joy, you will look at the world and get joy. You will also get peace and the feeling of oneness, universal oneness. If your heart centre is fully open, during meditation you are likely to taste the divine nectar, *amrita*.

Question: If you feel warmth in the region of the heart, is this a sign of the heart centre opening up?

Sri Chinmoy: If you feel heat and the rotation of a disc at the centre of the chest, then it is a sign that the centre is being opened. Doctors say that the physical heart is somewhat to the left of the chest, but the spiritual heart is in the middle of the chest. When the heart centre actually opens, its joy and delight will spread to the whole body so that you cannot actually say that it is located at any specific point.

Question: What is the relationship between the spiritual heart and the kundalini power in terms of relative importance?

Sri Chinmoy: Kundalini power, you can

say, is on the surface, absolutely on the surface of the spiritual heart. It is this way. On the surface of the sea are waves and all kinds of movement. When a child sees the waves of the ocean, he is so fascinated. But an adult will try to go deep within the ocean to where there is quiet and calm, absolute tranquility, for there he will get the greatest joy. The adult cares for the silent and eternal depths.

All the miracles that you may see from kundalini power are like the play of children in a garden. A child has the capacity to pick a flower or to pinch someone or to show how much strength he has by throwing a brick and doing all kinds of mischief. The Cosmic Mother observes the games of her children. Like an ordinary Mother, she enjoys having her children playing around her. "My children can jump, they can run, they can throw," she says. "Let us enjoy the game, the cosmic Game." But the Father feels that the children cannot go on playing all the time. They have to study sometimes or they will remain fools.

When a child is playing he is getting joy, physical joy. But when he studies he gets another kind of joy, a joy which is deeper and more fulfilling. On the physical plane, when somebody achieves something we appreciate him. If somebody does something great on the mental plane, we appreciate that person more. When somebody achieves something on the psychic plane, those who are in a position to appreciate him, appreciate him even more. And when somebody achieves something on the soul's plane, God's plane, those who know of it appreciate him most of all. Sri Ramana Maharshi did not care for study; Sri Ramakrishna did not care for study. There are many spiritual Masters who did not care for study. But all the scholars of the Western world should go and touch the feet of these illiterate men of infinite Wisdom. The higher, the deeper we go, the more convincing, the more illumining, the more worthwhile the wisdom we get. In the spiritual realm, kundalini power is like the achievement on the physical plane.

A mother feels that even if her son is sixty years old, he is still her young child, her baby. But when a father sees that his son is thirteen or fourteen years old, he immediately tries to give the son all his wisdom. He says, "You cannot call yourself a child any more. Tomorrow I may die and you will have to replace me and take full responsibility for all my jobs." The mother says, "No! No! No! I want my child to remain here with me." Now, I am not saying a word against the Mother. Only it is the Mother's nature to regard her sons as Her eternal children. The Father says, "You are eternal children, true; but you have to work for Me. You have to take the responsibility of the entire universe. Showing off and doing all these things is good for five years, ten years, twenty years, but it cannot last forever."

The same Mother, the same Cosmic Mother who holds all the Kundalini Power, who *is* the Kundalini Power, is far, far beyond it. With Her aspect of the ever-transcending Beyond, She is mixing with Her consort, Purusha, Shiva, or the Absolute. With Her ever-transcending Consciousness, She is one with the Absolute. Again, with Her playful consciousness, She is playing with Her children in Her cosmic Game.

The Father tells the child to go beyond the cosmic Game, for it is only when one goes beyond the cosmic Game that one will attain infinite Peace, Light and Bliss. The Father says, "You have to go beyond the Kundalini into a higher state of consciousness. First enter into the *sushupti,* the state of deep sleep. Then go into *swapna,* the dreaming state; then into *jagriti,* the waking state; and finally enter into *turiya,* the transcendental Consciousness. And, my children, you can even go beyond that and remain in *sahaja samadhi,* a constant, spontaneous and dynamic oneness with Me on all planes of Reality."

The son of God, Jesus Christ, was on earth for thirty-three years. Only during the last three years of his life did he perform miracles. But do you think the world still adores and worships him just because he could walk on water or resurrect a dead man? No, it is not because of his miracles that he is still worshippped, but because he brought down the eternal Consciousness, the infinite Consciousness. Sri Ramakrishna performed practically no miracles and there were many, many other spiritual Masters who did not do miracles. They felt that performing miracles on the physical plane would be childlike in comparison to what they were capable of doing on the spiritual plane, in the heart's region where infinite Peace, Light and Bliss abide.

Kundalini power and all the miraculous powers on earth are fleeting, for they are earth-bound powers. But the Power of the Self is infinite; the Power of the transcendental Self is infinite and immortal. The most important thing on earth for a spiritual seeker is the awakening of the consciousness and the realisation of the Self, for this is eternal. If somebody comes here and performs some miracles, we will be fascinated. But the moment we go home there will be nothing to sustain our faith in what he has done. It seems to be all magic and trickery. And how long can we cherish the magician inside us or before us? But when somebody lifts up our consciousness even for a second, or if we ourselves do it on the strength of our intense aspiration, then our faith in that experience lasts, because it is our own inner experience. Anything that lasts forever we need. It is Immortality, inner Immortality that we need; and this comes through the awakening and elevation of our consciousness.

Question: I have been meditating on my navel centre. Do you feel this is wise?

Sri Chinmoy: According to the strict Hindu system, this chakra should not be opened up until the heart centre is opened up. If the navel centre is opened before the heart, then the lowest vital, the most impure vital, may enter into the heart and destroy all your spiritual possibilities.

At this point in your spiritual development the navel centre is not a safe centre. It is the centre of dynamism, strength, power and so forth. You should meditate on your heart centre to get peace and love and joy. When you have peace, love and joy, you will feel that peace itself is power, love itself is power, joy itself is dynamic power. If you open the navel centre, where there is dynamism, and if you misuse this dynamism, it becomes brutal aggression. The navel centre is also the emotional centre. With this emotion you can expand yourself and become the Infinite. But again, when you start receiving the emotion of the navel centre, you may become a victim to pleasure, earthly pleasure, and human weakness. So God is not allowing you to open this centre. He is protecting you.

God does not want you to misuse the dynamic qualities which you have inside and around your navel centre. What He wants from you is the inner cry for Him. This inner cry is not here (in the navel) or here (in the throat) or here (in the third eye) or here (at the crown of the head). It is only in the heart. The one place to cry for God is here. If you really cry for God, no matter where you are or in which position you are, you are bound to feel God's Presence. And when you feel God's Presence, you can feel that the divine energy, the kundalini, is already awakened and is rising toward the highest. From one centre to another, it is going up, up, up. If you can feel God's living Presence inside you, this energy that you are speaking of will be yours in boundless measure in a very short span of time.

You cannot live without God; I cannot live without God. Everybody has to live with God, but to feel His living Presence is something else. Those who have realised God feel God's living Presence twenty-four hours a day. If you cry for that living Presence, your whole being, your inner existence and outer existence, will be flooded with divine dynamism and boundless energy.

Question: Then what about meditating on the base of the spine and trying to raise the kundalini from there. Is that also unsafe?

Sri Chinmoy: Some people very often make a mistake. They try to raise their kundalini in the traditional way, starting from the base of their spine; but their vital remains impure. Then they get into a lot of vital trouble. They say, "Oh, before Yoga I was far better off. I was very pure, but now my purity has all gone."

Question: Could you please speak about the fifth chakra?

Sri Chinmoy: The fifth chakra is the throat centre. It is called the vishuddha or kantha chakra. The Sanskrit word for throat is 'kantha'. Like the other chakras, vishuddha is inside the subtle body, inside the subtle physical and not in the gross physical.

When one opens this chakra, one is bound to create things. One can be a writer, one can be a singer, one can be a dancer. When this chakra is opened, it means that one has established a free access to the world of creativity. This centre has a special connection with the universal music. This universal music is totally different from the music that we play or hear. This music is celestial; we can't express it. We hear this music inside the heart centre, anahata. Our ordinary human ears can't hear it; with our inner ear we hear that music.

Expression, revelation and manifestation: these are pure imagination unless and until the fifth chakra is opened up. We can realise the Truth, but unless and until the Truth is revealed and manifested in this world, it is sheer imagination. In other worlds, in the inner worlds, it is a reality. But unless and until we see something right in front of our nose, we have every right to deny it. When the throat chakra is opened up, imagination is transformed into reality. What we call imagination is a reality in some other world. In another world, vision has its own reality in a divine way; but until it is transformed into reality in the outer world, we do not fully accept it. The moment the fifth chakra is opened up, anything that is within in potentiality will come forward for its own divine manifestation. So this centre is the centre of expression, revelation and manifestation of one's hidden inner Truth.

Question: They say that there are eighty-six thousand subtle nerves. Are they distinct enough to actually be counted?

Sri Chinmoy: Yes, the nerves are quite visible to the inner eye. They are not at all entwined; they are very distinct. But they are very light and delicate, very subtle. Once I tried to count them. I think that I counted two or three thousand and then I did not want to count any more. I said, "I believe it."

Question: Do the nerves of the subtle body have any correlation with the nerves of the physical body?

Sri Chinmoy: No. If you cut a physical nerve, the subtle nerve will not be affected at all. But you can bring messages from the subtle nerves into the physical; you can bring energy and other wealth from the subtle into the physical. The purpose of the subtle nerves is to give energy to the subtle physical. By your concentration you can strengthen your subtle nerves.

Sri Chinmoy was born in Bengal, India in 1931. While still a child he had many deep mystical experiences and at the age of twelve entered an ashram or spiritual community. Here he spent the next twenty years in intense prayer and meditation, perfecting his inner vision and reaching that rare state of oneness with God that various traditions call Enlightenment or God-realisation.

Sri Chinmoy would have been content to spend the rest of his life in a samadhi trance, maintaining only the thinnest connection with the physical world. But an inner command that he leave India and offer his realisations to aspiring humanity brought him to the United States ten years ago. Since then, Sri Chinmoy spiritual centres have been established throughout the U.S., Canada, Europe, Australia and the Far East and thousands have been drawn to his inner light.

Besides meditating for several hours a day and guiding his various centres, Sri Chinmoy conducts meditations twice a week for United Nations delegates and staff in New York. He delivers the monthly Dag Hammarskjold Lecture at the U.N. and is frequently invited to speak at major universities the world over. A prolific writer, Sri Chinmoy has published over two hundred books of spiritual poetry, aphorisms, essays, short stories and lectures. He is also a prolific artist, having completed more than ten thousand paintings and pen-and-ink drawings.

opening the third eye and other chakras. Sri Chinmoy also warns of dangers and pitfalls to be avoided and discusses some of the occult powers that come with the opening of the chakras.

paperback, $3.00

Sri Chinmoy Primer— Sri Chinmoy answers the kinds of questions that new disciples and seekers most frequently ask a spiritual Master. Subjects include meditation, diet, yogic breathing, the role of sex, how to choose a Guru and spiritual initiation.

paperback, $2.00

The Goal Is Won— A series of 360 poems written in the span of a single day through the use of yogic powers of concentration. The poems reveal the height, depth and vastness of the Seer-Poet's mystic vision.

paperback, $5.00

The Summits of God-Life: Samadhi and Siddhi— This book represents one of the very few genuine accounts of the universe beyond time and space. Sri Chinmoy here answers very specific questions on liberation, illumination, samadhi, Nirvana, transcendental Bliss and the different planes of Consciousness.

paperback, $3.00

Colour Kingdom—A Yogi of the highest order uses his spiritual vision to reveal the inner meaning and occult significance of different shades of colour. For each colour patch reproduced in the book, Sri Chinmoy tells its particular psychic quality and elaborates on this with an aphorism.

paperback, $5.00

Beyond Within—A 500-page anthology of essays, discourses, stories, poems and aphorisms collected from Sri Chinmoy's writings during his ten years in the West. In this book, an illumined yogi discusses topics such as the human psyche, meditation, will, consciousness and the higher worlds of Bliss and Light.

paperback, $6.95

For a catalogue of other books
by Sri Chinmoy, please contact:

Aum Publications
Box 32433
Jamaica, New York 11431